1/17

W9-BNU-804

Native Peoples of THE ARCTIC

By Lynda Arnéz

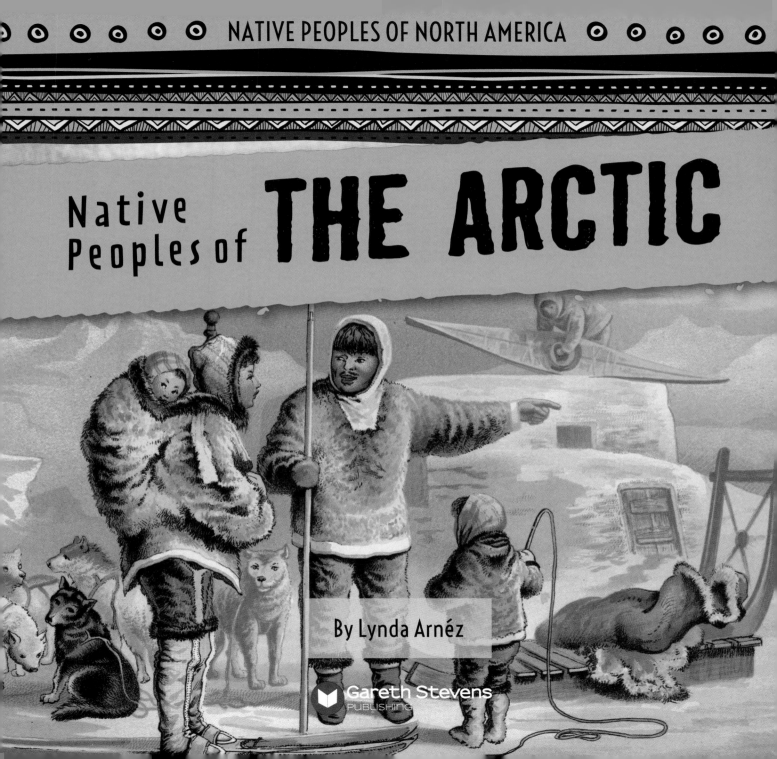

Gareth Stevens
PUBLISHING

Please visit our website, www.garethstevens.com. For a free color catalog of all our high-quality books, call toll free 1-800-542-2595 or fax 1-877-542-2596.

Library of Congress Cataloging-in-Publication Data

Names: Arnéz, Lynda, author.
Title: Native peoples of the Arctic / Lynda Arnéz.
Description: New York : Gareth Stevens Publishing, 2017. | Series: Native
  peoples of North America | Includes index.
Identifiers: LCCN 2015045646 | ISBN 9781482448221 (pbk.) | ISBN 9781482448078 (library bound) | ISBN
9781482447583 (6 pack)
Subjects: LCSH: Inuit–Arctic regions–History–Juvenile literature. |
  Indians of North America–Arctic regions–History–Juvenile literature.
Classification: LCC E99.E7 A7653 2017 | DDC 970.004/9712–dc23
LC record available at http://lccn.loc.gov/2015045646

First Edition

Published in 2017 by
Gareth Stevens Publishing
111 East 14th Street, Suite 349
New York, NY 10003

Copyright © 2017 Gareth Stevens Publishing

Designer: Samantha DeMartin
Editor: Kristen Nelson

Photo credits: Series art AlexTanya/Shutterstock.com; cover, p. 1 UniversalImagesGroup/Universal Images Group/
Getty Images; p. 5 (main) Christopher Wood/Shutterstock.com; p. 5 (map) AlexCovarrubias/Wikimedia Commons;
p. 7 (main) Photo 12/Universal Images Group/Getty Images; p. 7 (map) Peter Hermes Furian/Shutterstock.com;
p. 9 Science & Society Picture Library/SSPL/Getty Images; p. 11 Sergey Krasnoschokov/Shutterstock.com;
p. 13 Wolfgang Kaehler/LightRocket/Getty Images; p. 15 (main) Dmytro Pylypenko/Shutterstock.com; p. 15 (harpoon)
Werner Forman/Universal Images Group/Getty Images; p. 17 Fox Photos/Hulton Archive/Getty Images; p. 19 Apic/
Hulton Archive/Getty Images; p. 21 Andrew H. Brown/National Geographic/Getty Images; p. 23 Hulton Archive/Hulton
Archive/Getty Images; pp. 25, 29 (mask) Edward S. Curtis/Wikimedia Commons; p. 27 (main) Universal History Archive/
Universal Images Group/Getty Images; p. 27 (mask) Wellcome Images/Wikimedia Commons; p. 29 (duck) Ansgar
Walk/Wikimedia Commons; p. 29 (doll) McLeod/Wikimedia Commons.

Printed in the United States of America

CPSIA compliance information: Batch #CS16GS: For further information contact Gareth Stevens, New York, New York at 1-800-542-2595.

CONTENTS

Words in the glossary appear in **bold** type the first time they are used in the text.

Into the ARCTIC

The word "Arctic" calls to mind icy cold, snow, and long nights. Yet people have lived in the Arctic **region** of North America for thousands of years!

Every part of daily life for the native peoples of the Arctic was **adapted** to the conditions around them. Their homes and clothing were made to be warm and waterproof. They used the animal **resources** around them to the fullest. Most importantly, they worked together and valued people who used their skills to help the community survive in the cold.

In geography, "Arctic" means the area around the North Pole. It ends to the south at around 65°N **latitude**.

Greenland

Canada

■ =where Arctic peoples lived

United States

Mexico

The North American Arctic region covers part of present-day Canada and Alaska. Sometimes Greenland is included in this area, but this book will focus on the main part of North America.

ANCESTORS

Before about 20,000 years ago, Alaska and Siberia were connected by a land bridge called Beringia. The **ancestors** of the native peoples of North America left Asia and likely lived on this land for thousands of years. Then, as water began to cover it about 13,000 years ago, they crossed Beringia to North America.

Many of them went south to live in the warmer, more welcoming lands of the Great Plains, present-day California, and other parts of the modern United States. Others settled in the Arctic.

Today, about 4 million people live in the worldwide Arctic region. Many share common ancestors!

SIBERIA

ALASKA

BERINGIA

BERING SEA

The land bridge has been completely covered by water for thousands of years. It's now called the Bering Strait.

7

Grouped by LANGUAGE

The native peoples of the Arctic can be divided into three main groups based on their **traditional** languages. The Yupik, Aleut, and Inuit-Inupiaq speak somewhat different languages, but they're all **descended** from people who were part of the Eskimo-Aleut (or Inuit-Aleut) language family.

You may know the term "Eskimo." The native peoples of the Arctic don't want to be called that. Together, these groups are often just called the "Inuit." Their traditional lifestyles, homes, and communities are similar to one another.

The Inuit had to be able to count on one another to survive living so far north.

TELL ME MORE

"Eskimo" means "raw-meat eater." "Inuit" means "people" or "human beings."

9

Escaping the COLD

In the Arctic, there's no escape from the cold of winter. If you live on the coast, there are terrible snowstorms and rainstorms. Inland, it can drop to well below freezing, or 32°F (0°C).

As a result, many Arctic peoples lived nomadic lifestyles. "Nomadic" means they didn't stay in one place for very long. They traveled with the seasons to the best places to find food and stay away from the worst cold and weather. When caribou herds traveled south in the winter, the Inuit followed them.

TELL ME MORE

The native peoples of the Arctic often lived on the coasts during the winter and inland during the summer.

Caribou are members of the deer family. They were one of the most important animals hunted by the Inuit.

Building a HOME

Perhaps the best-known home of the Arctic peoples is the igloo. Igloos, however, were mostly built in the central Arctic and weren't the most common kind of home across this cold region.

Karmaks were built partly underground and had a round top. The frames were made of whale ribs and wood, then covered with earth. In spring and summer, many people of the Arctic made a tent of caribou skin or sealskin. They were easy to move and worked well for the Arctic peoples' nomadic life.

The tent Arctic peoples built for spring and summer was called a *tupik*, or *tupiq*.

TELL ME MORE

Igloos were built of blocks of snow and ice. Women and children would spend time filling in the little holes left between the blocks while men built a small tunnel entrance to the home.

The HUNT

People of the Arctic hunted all year long. Polar bear, musk ox, Arctic hare, and caribou were just some of the land animals they hunted.

Seals were hunted on the Arctic coasts. They make small holes in the ice so they can come up for air after diving deep to catch food. Hunters would look for these small holes. Then, when a seal surfaced at the air hole, the hunters would kill it with a long, sharp tool called a harpoon.

The native peoples of the Arctic used every part of the animals they hunted, from meat to bones and skin.

harpoon

When each animal was hunted depended on the season. Seals, for example, were most easily hunted between July and September.

Delicious **FISH**

Some Inuit lived along rivers in the Arctic. There, and also in the ocean, they fished for food, too. Artic char, whitefish, and trout were all eaten by the Inuit.

Harpoons were used to fish as well. Lines were tied to the harpoon, as well as floats made of sealskin. In the winter, the Arctic peoples made holes in the ice and dropped their lines into the water that way! Nets and spears were other fishing tools made and used by the Inuit.

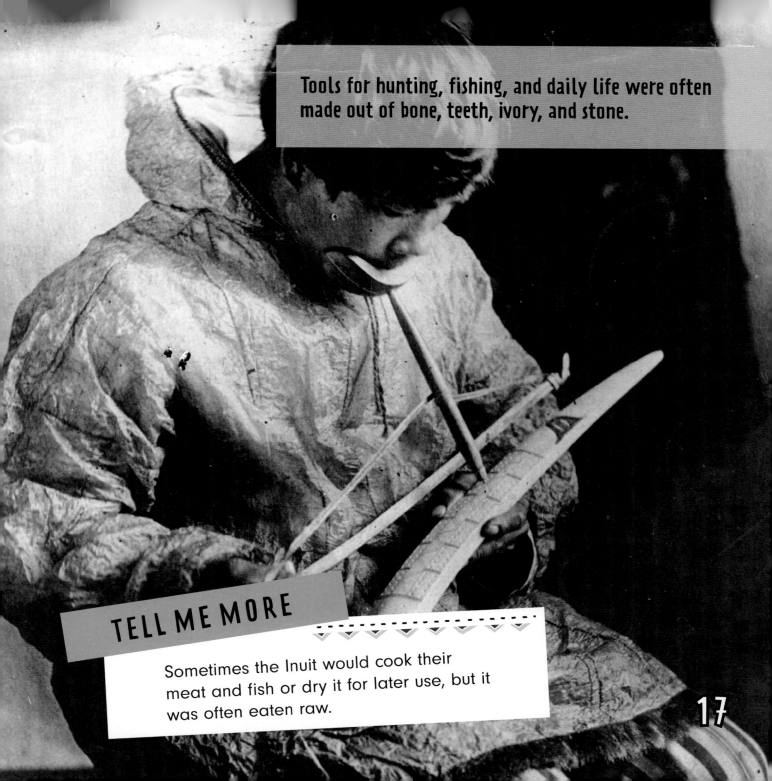

Tools for hunting, fishing, and daily life were often made out of bone, teeth, ivory, and stone.

TELL ME MORE

Sometimes the Inuit would cook their meat and fish or dry it for later use, but it was often eaten raw.

17

snowy **TRAVEL**

When moving over land during the winter, the Inuit sometimes traveled on foot. They wore boots made of several layers of animal skin to keep their feet warm and dry. Pointy pieces added to the bottom of their boots helped them walk on the ice and snow. They also traveled by sleds pulled by dogs.

During the summer when there was no ice covering Arctic waterways, native peoples used two kinds of boat. Kayaks were made for one person, and umiaks could hold about 10 to 15 people.

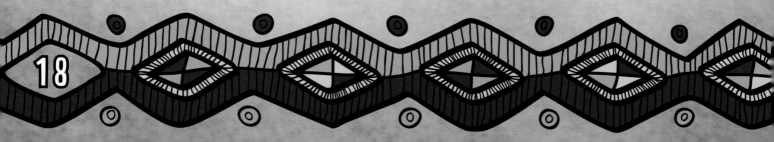

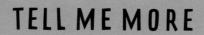

Umiaks were taken into the open ocean to hunt whales!

Kayaks were lightweight, watertight, and could move easily in the water.

19

Winter **WEAR**

Native peoples of the North American Arctic took great care in dressing for the cold. Clothing was similar for men and women. It was made of animal skin and fur, most commonly caribou, but also wolf, polar bear, bird feathers, and sealskin.

During the coldest months, the Inuit wore layers of mittens, boots, pants, and big coats called parkas. Often, the clothing had fur facing inside and another layer of fur facing out. They had snow goggles made of caribou **antlers**, too.

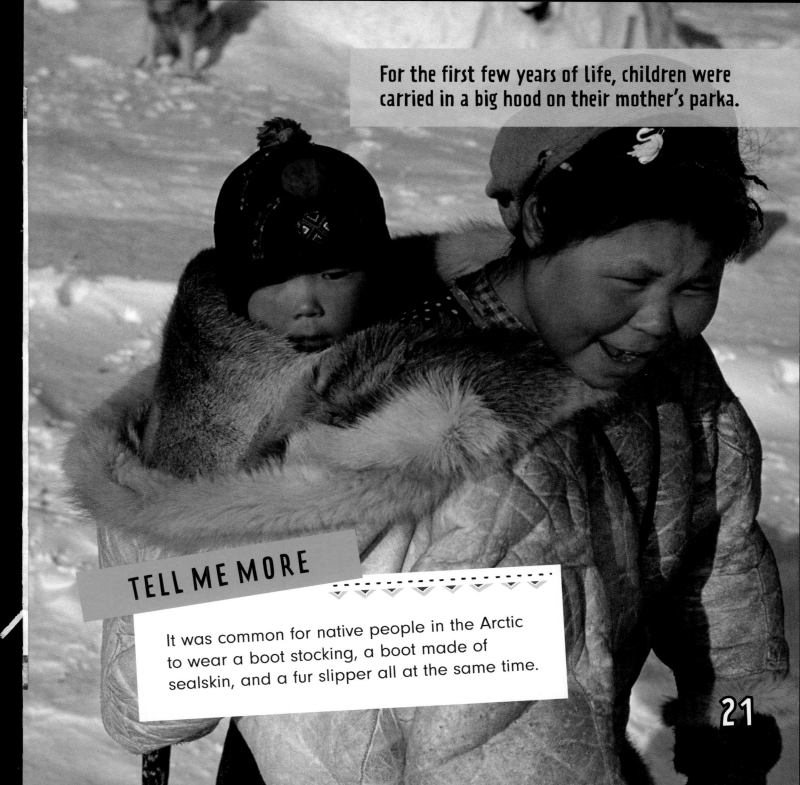

For the first few years of life, children were carried in a big hood on their mother's parka.

TELL ME MORE

It was common for native people in the Arctic to wear a boot stocking, a boot made of sealskin, and a fur slipper all at the same time.

Jobs TO DO

In the cold Arctic, men and women had to work together to survive. Their jobs were divided, but supported one another. In general, men built Inuit homes. They hunted and fished as well as made the tools used for hunting and fishing.

Women had the big task of making and repairing the warm Inuit clothing. They cooked and took care of children. Women also dressed the animal skins men brought home. That means they cleaned the skins for use.

The native peoples of the Arctic tended to be short and stocky, or solid looking. This allowed them to live in the cold with less heat loss from their body.

TELL ME MORE

Women used **sinew** from an ocean animal called the narwhal to sew clothing together. This was one way they made clothes waterproof.

ALL in the FAMILY

The peoples of the North American Arctic lived spread out from one another. The most important group was the family, commonly about five to six people. In the winter, a few families would live and hunt together, but in the summer they would go their separate ways.

A chief didn't often lead groups of Inuit. In fact, if someone started to have too much power, their family would pull them out of it. In general, there was very little government.

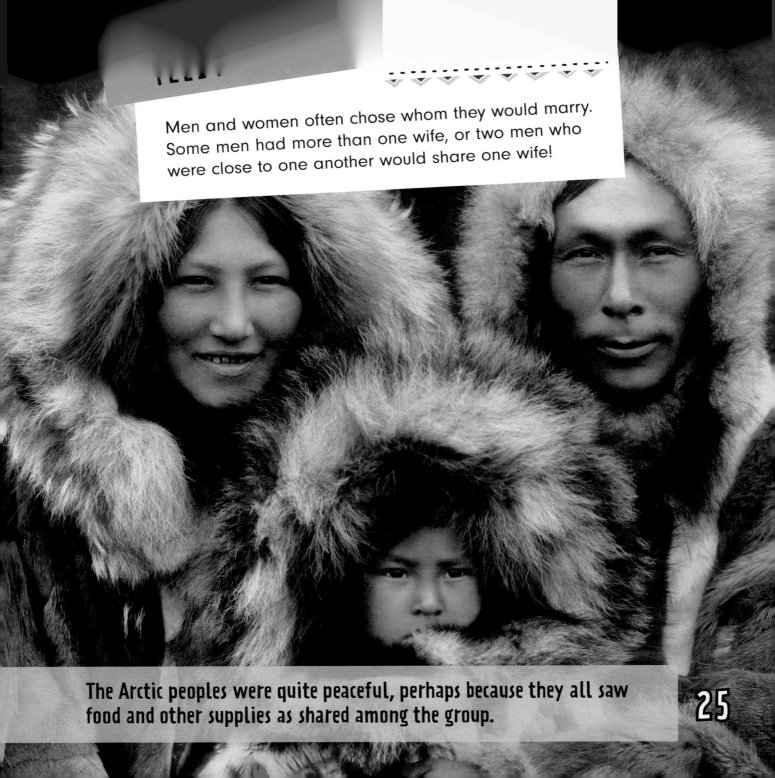

Men and women often chose whom they would marry. Some men had more than one wife, or two men who were close to one another would share one wife!

The Arctic peoples were quite peaceful, perhaps because they all saw food and other supplies as shared among the group.

The Spirit WORLD

The Inuit believed that everything had a spirit, whether it was alive or not. This is called animism. When something died, its spirit would go to live in the spirit world.

The second major Inuit belief was that special people called shamans were the only ones who could control the spirits. They wore masks and did dances to talk to the spirits. Then, they would tell others what to do to make the spirits happy, such as giving them gifts or moving on from a place.

The shaman's masks were made of wood or whalebone. They were often made to look like animals or to show people what the shamans saw in the spirit world.

TELL ME MORE

The Inuit followed certain rules for hunting and eating in order to keep the spirits happy.

CONTACT!

During the 1700s, the native peoples of the North American Arctic met their first outsiders. The Russian navy began making trips to Alaska to gather sea otter and seal fur. Many native peoples in the Arctic and subarctic region died fighting the Russians.

Today, many native peoples live much the same way you do in modern homes and with modern jobs! However, traditional ways of life still survive. In fact, many Inuit work together to save their **culture**'s arts, beliefs, and languages.

ART OF THE ARCTIC PEOPLE

Art, including shamans' masks and other **carvings**, is an important part of Inuit culture.

TELL ME MORE

Contact with Europeans came much sooner for the native peoples of Greenland. Around 1,000 years ago, people called the Norse traveled from Iceland to explore Greenland.

GLOSSARY

adapt: to change to suit conditions

ancestor: a family member who lived long before another

antler: the bony horn of an animal

carving: an object formed by cutting and shaping matter such as bone

culture: the beliefs and ways of life of a group of people

descend: to come after another person in a family

latitude: one of the imaginary lines that run east and west above and below the equator

region: a large area of land that has features that make it different from nearby areas of land

resource: a usable supply of something

sinew: a tough cord that comes from the muscle of an animal

traditional: having to do with long-practiced ways of life

For More INFORMATION

Books

Chesterfield, Jayson. *Inuit*. New York, NY: PowerKids Press, 2016.

Doak, Robin S. *Arctic Peoples*. Chicago, IL: Heinemann Library, 2012.

Kuiper, Kathleen, ed. *Indigenous Peoples of the Arctic, Subarctic, and Northwest Coast*. New York, NY: Rosen Educational Services, LLC, 2012.

Websites

Arctic

education.nationalgeographic.com/encyclopedia/arctic/

Learn even more about the Arctic region of Earth here.

Inuit Peoples

ducksters.com/history/native_americans/inuit_peoples.php

Do you want to know more about the Inuit? Find out more about their lives on this website.

INDEX